Workplace, Rumors, Lies, Social Loafing and Deviance

Louis Bevoc

Published by
NutriNiche System LLC

Rumors

Scope

The book examines rumors in organizations. It explores the reasons they occur, analyzes the effects they have on personnel, and suggests ways to reduce and control their presence. Examples are used for illustration and clarification, and the text is written so it is easily comprehended by readers at all levels.

Introduction

Rumors have been around as long as people have communicated. Although this statement is difficult to prove, most people know that it is true...especially if they have worked in an organization for any length of time.

Some workplace rumors are relatively harmless. They spread from one employee to another and are eventually forgotten or found to be untrue. Unfortunately, this is not the case for all rumors....and problems can result.

Workplace rumors can create warring factions among employees because workers take sides based on their perception of what might happen. Many times that perception does not turn into reality...but the damage has already been done.

Rumors can also cause employees to lose faith and trust in management. This is because most rumors have some type of negativity associated with them. For example, common themes of rumors often revolve around terminations (layoffs, firings, resignations, or retirements) or finances (raises, bonuses, profits, losses, or stability). Based on these two focal points, it is rather easy to see why rumors are often associated with bad occurrences. In short, negative happenings interest employees and that is why they move to the forefront of the rumor mill.

Problems associated with rumors are discussed in the effects section of this book. However, before moving to that section, let's first examine the reasons why rumors occur. In other words, what causes rumors to start? That question is answered in the next section.

Causes

Workplace rumors begin for a variety of different reasons because every worker does not process information the same. This is because employees:

- *Have different perceptions of situations*

    People in the same situation can have completely different perceptions of what is transpiring. Different perceptions affect rumors because they determine the amount of time and effort an employee will put forth discussing, analyzing, and inquiring about those rumors.

    Organizational example

A rumor is going around that the marketing department of a struggling automotive supplier is going to lay off ten people.

An accountant who works for a struggling auto supplier believes this reduction in work force is completely justifiable. After all, the company's financial situation does not justify maintaining people who are not directly contributing to the bottom line.

However, the accountant's perception is not shared by the salespeople. They believe marketing people are essential for advertising the company's products. Without marketing personnel, the salespeople believe the auto supplier will fare even worse financially.

- *Have different involvement in situations*

People in the same situation can have different involvement in that situation. This affects rumors because it determines people's emotional reaction to them.

Organizational example

A rumor is going around that the vice president of a candy company is going to be fired.

This is stressful for the niece and nephew of the candy company executive. They both work for the organization, and the vice president is key to their careers. His termination might be bad for their future advancement.

This means very little to other employees at the candy company. They do not wish any harm to the vice president, but his termination will likely not affect their jobs in any way.

- *Have different understanding of situations*

People in the same situation can have different understanding of that situation. This affects rumors because it determines people's concerns regarding them.

Organizational example

A rumor is going around that a national pharmaceutical manufacturer is going to lose a drug store chain as a customer.

The hourly production employees are not particularly worried about losing this customer. They know how much product they manufacture for that drug store, and it is relatively insignificant when compared to the total production volume of the company.

However, top management in the organization is very concerned about losing the drug store chain. They realize that this chain is the major reason that other stores buy their products, and losing this customer could result in a 40 percent drop in sales.

Based on the above information, it is understandable that every cause of rumors in organizations cannot be addressed in this book. However, the major causes are as follows:

Misinformation

This might be the most common cause of rumors in organizations. It happens when employees have inaccurate, insufficient, or incomplete information about an event or happening at work.

Organizational example

Sangeeta works in the office of a garage door installation company. She hears through the grapevine that the president is bringing in a financial consultant to monitor all employees' jobs and make suggestions for eliminating personnel.

Based on this information, Sangeeta tells the installation supervisors that their jobs might be in jeopardy. The supervisors notify their employees about this concern, and two of those workers leave the company for other positions rather than face the possibility of being laid off.

Unfortunately, Sangeeta did not have accurate information about this situation. The president is bringing in a financial consultant, but that person's sole responsibility is to prepare the company for an audit from their bank. The consultant is not doing any type of job analysis, and she is not going to recommend layoffs for anyone.

Sangeeta's misinformation led her to make statements that were not true. Her discussions with others made them unnecessarily apprehensive, and it caused two employees to quit their jobs. In short, her actions caused a rumor.

The above example shows how damaging misinformation can be in terms of rumors. People make statements based on information that is not entirely true, and those statements evolve and change as they spread from worker to worker. In a relatively short period of time, rumors begin to go around the organization...and their impact can be damaging.

Fear

Fear is a very powerful emotion. History has shown that dictators and cult leaders can advantageously use it to get people to behave in certain ways. People are afraid of what might happen, so they conform to the leader's demands.

Fear also works well as a catalyst for workplace rumors. It impels employees to make assumptions, say things that might not be true, and do strange things.

Organizational example

Martin is an assistant manager at a tire store. The owner has told him that he is in the process of selling the business to a competitor. This alarms Martin because he knows this competitor might eliminate his position after the takeover.

To save his job, Martin starts a rumor that his boss is going to lose his job after the new company establishes control. He thinks this action will get his boss to leave the company, thereby opening up another management position that Martin could fill.

Martin knows his strategy might be a longshot, but his fear leads him to think that he has to do something to protect his job. He believes his best chance for survival is to eliminate a management position at his employer...so he starts a rumor about his boss being terminated after the company is sold.

The above example shows how fear is a cause of rumors. People react to situations based on anxiety, alarm, fright, and panic...even though those reactions might not be justified.

Wishful thinking

Rumors that result from wishful thinking are originated by employees who want or desire something to happen. These people typically have a goal of helping themselves or hurting designated coworkers. In short, wishful thinkers start rumors to get something to transpire in the workplace.

Organizational example

Melissa is a stylist at an upscale hair salon. She dislikes another stylist named Nicholas because he "sucks up" to the owner Natalie. He tells Natalie to her face that her solon has the best reputation in the area, and it is the best place that he has ever worked. However, he complains about the salon and his job behind her back.

Melissa wants Natalie to see the "real" Nicholas, so she decides to start a rumor about him. She tells her coworkers that he is doing side work for one of the salon's competitors, and he is thinking of working for them full time. Melissa knows that this news will upset Natalie if it gets back to her, so she makes sure all of the employees hear it.

Melissa starts this rumor because she wants Natalie to know that Nicholas is a fake. He professes a love for his job and the salon when Natali is present, but his tone changes dramatically when she is not around. This rumor is unfair to Nicholas because it is not true, and it is a direct result of Melissa's wishful thinking due to his behavior.

The above example shows how wishful thinking can create rumors. This is typically not good for people or organizations...but it does happen, and it shows why rumors need to be prevented.

Boredom

Believe it or not, some employees start rumors simply because they are bored. They do not have enough work to keep them interested or motivated in their jobs, so they make statements that are not necessarily true to pass time and provide entertainment.

Organizational example

Lawrence is a salesperson at a car dealership. He is required to be at his job Monday through Friday, from 11:00 am – 7:30 pm. However, most customers do not start showing up to look at cars until about 4:00 pm, so his first five hours of every day are rather uneventful.

One slow afternoon, Lawrence tells everyone in the office that he has a friend who is going to open a local truck dealership. This new owner is going to hire a complete office staff...and he pays his employees very well. This excites the people in the office as they think about the possibility of switching companies for a higher wage.

In reality, Lawrence is not being completely truthful with his coworkers. He does have a friend who wants to open a local truck dealership, and he will need office employees. However, the deal is far from being completed, and Lawrence knows nothing about the wages the potential owner intends to pay his workers.

Lawrence starts this rumor because he is bored at the dealership. He wants to get everyone excited with interesting news...and he is successful in doing so. However, because he is not completely truthful about the situation, the end result is nothing more than a rumor.

Employees who spread rumors due to boredom are instigators who start fires with their comments. These individuals need more job-related work to do...or they should not be employed by the organization.

Deviance

This cause is actually more common than some people might think...and it is the most unacceptable reason for rumors. Employees say things they know are not factual to watch negative happenings unfold.

Organizational example

Mandy is an hourly production worker in the packaging department of a pet food manufacturer. She has been with the company for over ten years, but has never held a management position.

Recently, Mandy's supervisor left his job for a position at another organization. Mandy tells her coworkers that this supervisor was forced to leave because he stole money from the company. Not surprisingly, this story is interesting to everyone...and they spend a lot of time discussing it.

Unfortunately, Mandy spread a rumor about her former supervisor that had no truth. She made up the story about him stealing money simply to spread negativity about him throughout the workplace. This is wrong because it attacks a person who did nothing wrong, arouses emotions, and causes employees to waste time.

This cause for rumors is completely inexcusable because employees are well aware that they are spreading information that is not true. They do this to purposely cause problems in workplaces. They are not searching for entertainment...they simply just want to stir emotions and inflict pain on others.

Now that you are aware of some of the major causes of rumors, it is time to explore their impact. The next section does this by examining the effects rumors have on workplaces.

Effects

Many organizations do nothing about rumors. Management believes they are a normal aspect of the workday, and they are typically harmless. Unfortunately, this is not always true. Some rumors cause major problems if they are allowed to take root and develop, and the following are some of those problems:

Wasted time

Employees involved with rumors sometimes become so engulfed in them that a good portion of their day is spent discussing, analyzing, and inquiring about them. Please consider the following regarding these three aspects:

Discussing

Rumors have the potential to affect everyone in the organization. Because of this, they inspire a wealth of discussion among employees. Discussions are great for work-related issues because multiple minds combine to generate new thoughts and ideas. However, discussions that revolve around rumors do little more than waste time.

Analyzing

Employees waste time by meeting with each other and dissecting rumors that they have heard. They analyze those rumors and propose various "what if" scenarios so they can determine what might happen if they are true.

Analysis is great for problem-solving because it allows people to break down various aspects of issues for detailed evaluation. However, when the problems stem from rumors that are yet to be proven true, analysis is little more than a waste of time.

Inquiring

Sometimes it is not enough to simply analyze all information available regarding a rumor. Employees want to know more because they fear what might transpire, so they question coworkers who might have additional knowledge.

Inquiry is natural for all human beings because they seek to know more about things that impact their lives. However, in terms of rumors, inquiring minds end up wasting time.

Organizational example

Nolan is an inventory control manager at the distribution center for a clothing store chain. He recently heard a rumor that the company is going to fire two vice presidents and replace them with two people from one of their major competitors.

This rumor is very interesting to Nolan. He is naturally drawn to gossip, and this gossip is huge. Both vice presidents have been with the company for over 20 years, and are highly respected in the retail clothing industry. Their terminations would send shock waves through the organization, and employees would be left wondering why the company took such drastic action.

Nolan's intense interest causes him to ask his coworkers if they have more information about the rumor. In fact, he is so infatuated, that he draws up a spread sheet that shows the strengths and weaknesses of each vice president. He then lists potential replacements and analyzes which ones have legitimate shots at the positions that will be vacated. Unfortunately, all of this is done during working hours while Nolan neglects his inventory management responsibilities.

It is rather obvious that Nolan is wasting time on this rumor. He is far too involved in something that might not be true, and he is not doing the job he is paid to do while he gathers information. Leadership at the organization would not approve of his behavior because it does little to help the clothing distributor grow and prosper.

Based on the above, it is quite apparent that rumors lead to wasted time. When people waste time, they are not performing the tasks that they were hired to do...and this is not good for the employees or the organizations.

Unwarranted stress

Rumors cause employees to worry, and worry leads to stress. This stress can lead to major problems including:

Mistakes

It is easy for employees to make mistakes when they are experiencing stress. They think about the issues that are causing them stress, rather than their jobs. When they perform the various tasks related to their jobs, their minds drift off as they worry...and they ultimately make mistakes.

Unfortunately, these mistakes are made for reasons that do not even make sense. Employees do not know what is going to happen and are unsure if the rumors are factual...so they are essentially worrying about things that might never happen and might be based on fictitious information.

Mental health deterioration

When stress from rumors is too much, it wears on people. They look tired and feel exhausted. When they go to bed at night, they are kept awake thinking about the issues that are bothering them. In the morning, they wake up well short of refreshed and have to deal with another stressful day.

Stress from rumors also causes employees to become irritable and hostile. They experience difficulties that they can't seem to overcome, and their unpleasantness toward coworkers is a natural side effect. This hostility can be directed toward anyone without warning...and it is rarely justified. In fact, most times this type of behavior is based solely on the fact that the person is feeling the effects of the rumor mill.

Absenteeism

Some employees who experience stress would rather not deal with it, so they call in sick. They cannot handle rumor drama, so they choose not to by staying home.

This type of behavior can get worse if is not addressed. People who miss a lot of time from work might decide to leave permanently...or they might be terminated by their employer. This is discussed in more detail later in this section (see *depleted workforces*).

Organizational example

Sheryl works at a bank as a branch manager. She recently heard from employees at the corporate office that the bank is going to reorganize. All branch manager positions are going to be eliminated, and current branch managers will be made teller supervisors.

This change would not be good for Sheryl. Teller supervisors make 25 percent less money than branch managers, and she cannot afford to take the pay cut. She is a single mother who needs the income to support her two children.

Sheryl is very upset by the rumor, and she has trouble focusing on her job responsibilities. She makes mistakes that she has not made in the past, and the other employees start to notice. She feels tired during the work day and needs to take more frequent breaks from her daily tasks. Additionally, her stomach is upset when she wakes up in the morning, causing her to call in sick for a few days. Sheryl has never had an issue with absenteeism in the past, but she does not feel well enough to deal with the responsibilities of her job.

Sheryl is stressed over the thought that she might lose her current position. This causes her to make errors, experience fatigue, and call in sick due to physical health issues. In reality, Sheryl does not know what is going to happen...but the rumor mill has caused her to worry about a situation that could be very bad for her.

The worst part about stress created by rumors is the fact that it is unnecessary. The truth of the rumors has not been determined, so people could be worrying for no legitimate reason. However, employees' perceptions are their reality...and they perceive rumors to be fact so they experience stress.

Lowered productivity

This problem often results from the time that is wasted when employees involve themselves with rumors. Workers spend more time entrenched in rumors, and less time on their jobs....which makes them less productive. This leads to issues including:

Lost focus

People underestimate the power of focus in terms of doing the best job possible. Without it, mediocrity sets in as productivity decreases....and management settles for less than employees are capable of contributing. In short, focus is important for the survival and growth of organizations.

When rumors persist, employees are unable to concentrate on their jobs. They struggle to complete daily tasks, and critical aspects of work such as innovation and creativity are put on the backburner. "Gaining" gives way to "maintaining" as workplaces battle to sustain a break-even status.

Unfortunately, lost focus is typically the most common negative effect of workplace rumors. Employees concentrate on the rumor instead of their jobs and productivity suffers.

Lack of goal attainment

Goals are necessary for every workplace. Without them, organizational objectives cannot be achieved and growth and prosperity are limited. When employees are involved with rumors, they fail to accomplish designated goals.

Lower profitability

This is a natural progression because lower productivity typically results in lower profitability. Over time, the bottoms lines of organizations are negatively impacted by the rumors that swirl around them.

Organizational example

Tyreek works as an account manager for a local magazine. A manager in the office tells him that she believes the company will be giving bonuses at the end of the year that are two to three times as much as they were last year.

This rumor intrigues Tyreek because he would like to buy some property down south, and the extra bonus money would help him make that purchase. He calls the other account managers to tell them about the information he has obtained. This news excites everyone, and several employees decide to leave work early to meet at a bar and discuss the matter further.

The rumor Tyreek heard is good for the morale of the account managers, but it does little for the bottom line of the magazine. These employees lose focus on their jobs as they think about the money that they might receive. Their bar meeting during normal working hours means that they are socializing instead of selling. In this case, positive thoughts regarding a rumor that may or may not be true have lowered productivity of the account managers, thereby preventing them from achieving sales goals.

Lowered productivity is the most interesting effect of workplace rumors. In the beginning, it appears to be rather unimportant. It is not readily noticeable because productivity lowering is a slow process. However, over time it becomes more obvious because the bottom line of the organization is negatively impacted...and this means that some type of corrective action is needed.

Damaged reputations

Rumors can do serious damage to employees' reputations if personal and professional aspects of their lives are attacked. This leads to several negative feelings including:

Anger

Rumors can cause employees to become angry, especially if they are not true. Workers become even angrier if they try to set the facts straight...only to find that the rumors continue to persist.

Embarrassment

Embarrassment is different than anger. Like anger, it is a negative emotion...but it differs from anger because people feel uncomfortable rather than mad. Rumors embarrass employees when they cause them discomfort due to the perceptions their coworkers have of them.

Defensiveness

Anger and embarrassment can both result in employees becoming defensive. They do not want to look bad in the eyes of their coworkers, so they take a stance to protect themselves. Unfortunately, this type of behavior makes them look even worse in many situations...so their defensive actions are often futile.

Organizational example

Penelope is a stewardess at an airline. A rumor going around that she is having an affair with a pilot at the airline.

This rumor infuriates Penelope because it is not true. She is happily married and is embarrassed by the thought that anyone would think she would have an extramarital affair. She makes it very clear to everyone at the airline that she is loyal to her husband and family, and she becomes visibly upset if anyone does not appear to completely support her claim.

Some of the airline employees are surprised by Penelope's defensiveness. They realize the is upset by the rumor, but they do not understand why she feels compelled to plead her case to everyone...even employees who know nothing about it.

The affair rumor about Penelope caused her to become angry, embarrassed, and defensive. She was visibly upset, and her reaction disrupted the workplace for reasons that were not completely understood by other employees.

Damaged reputations cause employees to react emotionally due to their personal involvement. Some people become so upset that they leave their organization...as is discussed in the next section.

Depleted workforces

Some employees become emotionally distraught by rumors. If they cannot resolve this negativity, they sometimes leave their organizations.

Rumors produce the following negative feelings that lead to employees leaving organizations:

Panic

Rumors can cause employees to panic due to fear. They are afraid that the rumors might be true, so they seek safety at an organization that they believe is more stable.

Dejection

Rather than fight, some people choose to switch...even if they know they are right. Their name has been "dragged in the mud" and they want to free themselves from the damage caused by the rumors.

Disdain

Most people do not want to work in a continual rumor mill. They accept gossip as an occasional occurrence, but it becomes unbearable when there is constant drama.

When issues associated with rumors become too severe, some employees choose to leave for other employment. Quite simply, they do not want to deal with the avalanche of rumors...so they make a permanent change.

Organizational example

Florence works as an accountant at an office supply company. She enjoys her job for the work aspect of it, but she is tired of the endless office drama that continually surfaces due to rumors.

These rumors range from details of employees' personal lives to the financial stability of the company. Florence tries not to get involved in them, but this is virtually impossible because her desk is in the middle of an office of employees who thrive on gossip.

After a while, Florence can no longer deal with the never-ending rumor mill. She finds another job, gives her boss her notice of resignation, and happily leaves the office supply company.

Some employees want to do their jobs with as little drama as possible. They work to the best of their ability, but they have no interest in rumors...and they choose to leave organizations rather than deal with those rumors on a daily basis.

Now you understand some of the major effects of rumors. Since none of these are good, organizations need to manage the frequency and severity of rumors. Methods for that management are discussed in the next section.

Reducing and controlling

It is fairly safe to assume that rumors are never going to completely go away. Many people like hearing them, and they cannot resist getting involved. However, the frequency and severity of workplace rumors can be controlled. This is done by adhering to the following guidelines (also known by the acronym COARE):

Communicate

Keep lines of communication open. Let employees know what is happening so they do not have to guess to understand. Information needs to be communicated in good and bad times...and it must be clear.

Communicating can be done in a variety of different ways. Examples include meetings, newsletters, memos, letters, websites, emails, and blogs. The key is to make the communication real, honest, and consistent.

Observe

Watch what is going on and make mental notes by assessing the situation for problems. If there are patterns, then record those patterns so plans can be made to prevent them from reoccurring. Watch for individual employees who might start rumors so their behavior can be addressed.

This observation should not fall on the shoulders of specific management personnel in the organization. All supervisors need to be watching and recording rumor activities so they preventative action can be planned. In short, the combined effort of monitoring does a lot to prevent rumors from surfacing and prospering.

Avoid

Many people in management live by the "do as I say, not as I do" philosophy. They break rules that they expect others to follow because they believe they are exempt. Sometimes they actually are exempt because other employees lack the power or courage to do anything about their behavior...but it does not go unnoticed.

In terms of rumors, the "do as I say, not as I do" action is a terrible method of prevention. Managers who get involved with rumors are setting a bad example that other employees will surely follow. In short, management needs to avoid a "do as I say, not as I do" mentality by not becoming an active part of rumors.

React

Rumors move at an alarming speed, and they change rapidly as they spread from employee to employee. Because of this, management must act swiftly when rumors surface. They need to address the underlying causes, note the facts, and eliminate fears and concerns. The point is to help employees learn the truth by bringing things into the open. Unfortunately, this might require disciplinary action if the root cause stems from certain employees.

Explain

Justify the reaction phase. Be honest about why the swift action was taken. Employees who understand the reasons behind management decisions will be more committed to those decisions.

Additionally, expand on the explanation by telling employees that rumors are not acceptable in the workplace. Inform them about the damage that can be done by rumors, and give examples of some of the negative effects. Let them know what is being done to prevent rumors from starting...and what will happen to workers who engage in them.

Explanations help employees to understand the problems associated with rumors. This educates them and leads them to monitor their own actions.

Summary

Rumors have the potential to devastate workplaces. They result in wasted time, unnecessary stress, lower productivity, damaged reputations, and depleted workforces. That being said, rumors need to be controlled so their destruction is minimal.

This book examines rumors in organizations. It looks at the causes and effects of these workplace happenings, and it suggests ways to contain them. Real-world examples are used throughout the text for clarification and explanation, and the book is written so it is easily understood by readers at all levels.

Congratulations! You now know more about workplace rumors...and an important aspect of organizational behavior.

Lies

Introduction

The term "lie" is typically perceived by people as negative, and that perception is often for good reasons. Lies are incorrect, misleading, or false statements purposely made by people for some type of benefit or gain. Based on this definition, it's easy to understand the negative association.

Lies might be a purposeful distortion of the truth, but not all of them are considered deceitful or wrong. Some lies are accepted...and others are expected. Below are examples of each:

Accepted

You walk into the house of a friend who has just redecorated. You tell her that the decor looks nice even though you really do not like it. Your husband knows that you dislike the change, but he accepts your lie because he understands that you do not want to offend your friend by saying something negative.

Expected

Your friend Samuel tells you confidentially that is not going to church today because he has decided to go to a baseball game. When the pastor asks you if you know why Samuel is not at the service, you reply that you do not know. Samuel expects you to lie because he knows the truth could cause him problems with the pastor.

Lies are quite common in organizations. Employees purposely make incorrect, misleading, or false statements for some type of benefit or gain. They might want to make themselves appear better, make others look worse, avoid blame for something, or help someone else. Regardless of the reason, lies occur in workplaces on a fairly regular basis.

Like the personal examples above, employee lies are also not all considered deceitful or wrong because some are accepted and others are expected. Please consider the following examples:

Accepted

You visit a customer that has just installed a new inventory control program. You tell the purchasing agent that you think the program will work well for their operation, even though you had a negative experience with the company that sold it to them. Your boss knows that you dislike that particular company, but he accepts your lie because he understands that you do not want to offend a customer by saying something negative.

Expected

Your coworker Jennifer tells you confidentially that is not going to work today because she has decided to go to a concert. When your boss asks you if you know why Jennifer is not at work, you reply that you do not know. Jennifer expects you to lie because she knows the truth could cause her problems with the boss.

Anyone who has dealt with liars at work knows that they can cause a lot of problems. Lying is a form of dishonesty that needs to be managed before it gets out of hand, and the best way to manage it is to understand why it is occurring. This leads to the next section on reasons for employee lying.

Reasons

This section discusses reasons employees lie, and it presents some challenges because those reasons are virtually endless. It's difficult to list every motive for lying because that list is extremely broad and diverse. Employees lie for very understandable reasons, but they also make untrue statements that make no sense to anyone other than themselves.

Since the depth and scope of this book is limited, reasons for employee lying are generalized in the list below using organizational examples for better understanding.

Employees are trying to find happiness

Some people do not like their jobs. They are so unhappy that they attempt to find happiness by making statements about their planned actions without having any real intention of following through. For example, they say they are going to quit and tell the boss to "take the job and shove it." They also state that they are going to write a letter to the president of the company to expose all the wrongdoing in the workplace.

In reality, these employees are misleading others about their plans. They make unwarranted statements because they are upset with their jobs and believe lying about their intentions will make them feel better.

Organizational example

Sebastian works on a production line at a produce plant. His job is to put lettuce in boxes and stack the boxes on pallets...and he does not enjoy the work. He has tried to find employment elsewhere, but he has not been successful.

Sebastian is angry at the company because he feels stuck in his position. He believes he is capable of performing a higher-skilled job that pays more money, but no organization is willing to give him a chance. Since he cannot control his current situation, he periodically tells other employees that he "is going to quit" and "is done after today." He also says that he is "going to the president's office after work to let him know what is really going on."

Sebastian has never done what he said he is going to do. He has worked at the produce plant for three years and has never quit or requested a meeting with the president. He lies about what he is going to do because he is not satisfied with the work he performs.

Sebastian attempts to reduce his misery at work by making statements about what he is going to do...but he does not follow through on those statements. In short, he lies about his future actions and hopes that this will help him find happiness in his current position. Unfortunately, that happiness is not easily attained, and Sebastian's dishonesty is not successful.

Employees are trying to control others

Employees who want to control others often use threats for coercion. Sometimes those threats are carried out when coworkers do not comply with demands, but other times nothing is done. Threats that are not carried out are considered lies because the employees that made them were not being truthful about their intended actions.

Threats pose an interesting dilemma because it is often difficult to determine which ones are truthful and which ones are lies. This is because some threatened employees comply based on fear of the consequences, and then it is unknown whether or not those consequences would have actually been carried out. Credibility of threats can only be determined when employees refuse to comply.

Organizational example

Veronica works as a cashier at Janet's Discount Grocery Store, and she can scan 31 items per minute at the register. This is very good because the average cashier in the store scans 22 items per minute.

Rachael is also employed as a cashier at Janet's Discount Grocery Store. She is only able to scan 17 items per minute, and management wants her to increase her speed. This upsets Rachael, and she blames Veronica for causing her problem.

Rachael is a personal friend of the head cashier Natalie, and she uses this friendship to threaten Veronica. She tells Veronica that she needs to slow down her scanning or she will convince Natalie to "get rid of her."

Veronica ignores Rachael's threat and continues to work at a fast pace. She is complemented for her effort by Natalie, and there is no mention of firing her or eliminating her job. Veronica does not hear anything else from Rachael, and she soon realizes that Rachael never discussed her scanning speed with Natalie.

Rachael threatened Veronica to get her to comply and slow down her scanning. This threat did not work, and Rachael did not attempt to convince Natalie to terminate Veronica. In short, Rachael lied about her intended actions to try to gain control over Veronica. She gambled, and she lost.

Employees are trying to lie

Believe it or not, some employees lie simply for the sake of lying. They do not necessarily have a motive, and they are not trying to manipulate others. They are just prone to lie...regardless of the situation. These employees are known as compulsive liars.

The worse part about compulsive liars is the fact that some of them find it very difficult to break their habit. Their perpetual lying can affect work relationships and even lead to their termination, but they simply do not know how to stop.

Organizational example

Ryan works as a maintenance person at a horse racetrack. He does his job well, but he is not a truthful person. He fabricates stories, embellishes details, gives false information, and misleads other employees. On more than one occasion he has said (1) he completed projects when he did not, (2) he talked to the owner about making changes when he did not, and (3) he did not receive work orders for maintenance repairs after they were placed on his desk.

The worst part about Ryan's lying is much of it makes no sense. He has told coworkers (1) he does not each lunch when he has been seen bringing a lunch to work on several occasions, (2) he does not like music when it is heard coming from his car many on many days, and (3) he is a vegetarian when he has been seen eating steak. These matters do not appear to be important enough to lie about, but Ryan thinks otherwise.

Ryan's coworkers refer to him as "lyin' Ryan" because he seems to never tell the truth. They do not trust anything he tells them based on his history of false and misleading statements. In short, Ryan is a compulsive liar who is prone to lie regardless of the situation.

Employees are trying to get attention

Some employees like attention, and lies are a good way to attract it. These individuals fascinate coworkers by exaggerating or embellishing statements or stories, and this allows them to become a focal point for conversation. Employees guilty of this type of lying often continue to manipulate facts in an attempt to keep themselves at the center of attention.

Organizational example

Paul is employed as a salesman at an automobile dealership, and he likes to make up stories about his personal experiences. He discusses travel to destinations that he has never been to, talks about his customers' personal lives when he has never socialized with them outside of work, and chats about the medical schools his daughter is applying to after she changed her plan to become a doctor.

Paul fabricates stories because he likes when his coworkers listen to him speak. He enjoys being the focal point of conversation, and this is accomplished by embellishing his life experiences. In short, Paul lies to attract attention.

Employees are trying to attain higher status

Some employees want to be perceived as having higher social status than actually is the case, and they manipulate facts to establish that perception. They lie about the property they own, people they know, or money they possess to make others think that there are wealthy, important, or powerful.

The worse part about this type of liar is it can lead to more serious dishonesty. Theft and fraud can occur as employees strive to live the lifestyle that they attempt to portray. This negatively impacts coworkers and organizations, and it can also lead to legal action.

Organizational example

Melvin is a shift supervisor at an upholstery manufacturer. He earns a respectable salary, but he is not satisfied with being middle class. He wants to be perceived as rich because he believes rich people have influence and power.

To appear wealthy, Melvin lies about his material possessions. He claims to have two classic cars worth over $100,000 in his garage at home, but he does not drive them to work for fear that they might get damaged. He also says he owns a home up north on a few hundred acres that is worth over $300,000, but he never goes to it because he rents it out to some family members. Last, and most ludicrous of all, he states that he has a collection of Beatles' music, autographs, concert posters, and other memorabilia that is worth over $600,000...but none of his coworkers have seen this collection because it is stored in an undisclosed location for "security reasons."

Some employees, especially new ones, believe Melvin when he talks about his wealth. Over time, however, most people figure out that he is lying. This causes many employees to not believe him about work-related tasks that have nothing to do with his money. In short, Melvin's lies about his financial status cause coworkers to doubt everything he says.

Employees are trying to avoid responsibility for mistakes

Most employees do not like to get blamed for problems, especially when it is not their fault. However, there are times when blame is correctly placed on someone in the workplace. Some workers cannot handle that blame and they will do anything to avoid it...and that includes lying.

There are two basic ways employees lie to avoid taking responsibility for their mistakes. These are:

Blame others

This happens when employees falsely blame others for mistakes that they made, and it is the most common way workers lie to avoid responsibility. They simply pick a scapegoat and place the blame on him or her. Some workers are skilled at this and make sure they cover their tracks, while others are much more transparent with their actions. Either way, this type of action is very upsetting to those getting wrongly accused, and it causes workplace problems.

Deny involvement

This happens when employees falsely deny that they had anything to do with the mistake they made. They often act as if they have no understanding of what has happened. If pressed further, they deny any knowledge of the mistake to avoid taking responsibility. Some workers are much better at this than others due to experience...and those individuals are the most dangerous in terms of negatively impacting the workplace.

Organizational example

Molly and Adrian are CPAs at an accounting firm. Every CPA at the firm stores data in the same computer system so they can access each other's files if necessary. Molly mistakenly deletes a file belonging to a client of Adrian, and she is unable to recover it. She knows Adrian will be upset if she tells him about her error, so she decides to remain silent.

A few days later, Adrian needs the file that Molly deleted. He is visibly upset that he cannot find it and asks everyone in the office if they know what happened to it. Everyone, including Molly, denies any knowledge of the missing file.

Adrian searches in vain for the file, and he eventually realizes that it needs to be replaced. He contacts the client and asks her to resend all of her information. This annoys the client, and she is concerned about Adrian's carelessness. After thinking the matter over, she decides to use a different accounting firm for her taxes.

Molly denied any involvement with this problem. She lied about her error and got away with it. However, she caused some workplace problems due to her dishonesty. Adrian was stressed and did unnecessary work looking for a file that no longer existed, and the accounting firm lost a client.

Employees are trying to protect coworkers

This is the most interesting type of employee lying because it differs from others. The only benefit for the offending employees is that they helped a coworker in need. This can happen when:

Employees befriend coworkers

When employees establish friendships with coworkers, they do not want to see bad things happen to them. Based on this, they sometimes lie to protect them.

Organizational example

Jerry and Eleanor work as card dealers at a casino. They have established a friendship and spend time with each other's families outside of work.

The casino manager is Harold, and he asks Jerry if Eleanor is taking excessive time on her breaks. Jerry tells him she is not, even though this is not the truth.

Jerry knew Eleanor was taking too much time on her breaks. However, she is a friend, and he did not want to see her get into trouble. He lied to Harold to protect her.

Employees witness injustice done to coworkers

When employees see their coworkers treated unfairly, they want to help them find justice. Workers who lie in this type of situation find it easy to justify their actions.

Organizational example

Barry and Connie are bank tellers who both work for a manager named Wanda. Wanda treats Barry differently that the other tellers. She micromanages him and watches his every move. She also reprimands him for every mistake and does not accept any of his excuses for action or lack of action.

One day, Barry mistakenly misplaces the key to a customer's deposit box in the wrong safe. When Wanda discovers the key, she is upset. She suspects Barry, but she asks all the tellers if they know why the key was misplaced. Connie tells Wanda that she personally made the mistake and apologizes. Wanda accepts her apology and tells her to be more careful in the future.

Connie did not like the way Wanda treated Barry and did not want to see him get in trouble, so she took the blame for something she did not do. She lied and felt justified for her dishonesty.

Employees feel empathy toward coworkers

When employees see coworkers in difficult situations beyond their control, they feel empathy toward them and want to help.

Organizational example

Doug and Marlene are both supervisors in the shipping department of an online retail distribution center. They both report to Jamie, who is the distribution manager.

Marlene is a single parent who has two children under the age of three at home. She sometimes has difficulty getting to work on time because her babysitter shows up late.

Jamie wants all employees to be punctual, and she asks Doug if Marlene has been showing up late for work. Doug lies and says Marlene is always on time.

Doug knew that Marlene occasionally shows up late for work. However, he felt empathy because her situation was out of her control, so he lied when he was questioned by Jamie.

Employees are trying to maintain good coworker relationships

Some employees lie because they do not want to offend or upset coworkers for fear that it might damage their relationship. The benefit for dishonest employees is they maintain peace at work and are likely to get cooperation from others based on their lies.

Organizational example

Matt works in the quality control department at a pickle factory. He started with the company as a production employee seven years ago, and he has worked in his current position for the past four years.

Matt is highly respected in the organization because he works well with everyone while getting his job done. Helen, the plant manager, values his opinion about many aspects of plant operations. She asks him what he thinks about products, processes, procedures, and people.

Helen asks Matt about the productivity of a production line employee named Renee. Matt does not think Renee is very good in terms of productivity, but she keeps him abreast of quality issues on the line...and he does not want to jeopardize this relationship. Based on his rapport with Renee, Matt lies to Helen by telling her that Renee is a good worker.

Matt lied about Renee's productivity because she provides him with valuable information for his job. He was able to maintain a good working relationship with her, but he also gave false information about her productivity that could negatively impact the productivity of the pickle factory.

Employees are trying to maintain good customer relationships

This type of lying often protects the best interests of the employee and/or the company...but it still involves dishonesty. Many salespeople are guilty of this because they do not want to lose business.

Organizational example

Megan is an office supply salesperson. She reports to Bernard, the owner of the company, and he is a stickler about getting paid on time by customers.

Lisa owns nine pet supply stores and she furnishes her corporate office with supplies she buys from Megan. She has been late on paying her bills for the past three months, and Bernard tells Megan that Lisa needs to pay on time or she will be put on COD.

When Lisa's next bill is due, the check does not arrive. Bernard calls Megan and tells her to put Lisa on COD. However, Megan lies and tells Bernard that Lisa has given her the check. She immediately goes to Lisa's office, tells her the situation, and gets a check which she promptly hand delivers to Bernard.

Megan lied that she had Lisa's check to prevent her from being put on COD. She did this to satisfy Bernard and maintain a good relationship with a customer.

Now you understand some of the major reasons why employees lie. You also know that lying can cause problems in workplaces. This leads to a question. How can employee lying be prevented? That question is explored in the next section.

Prevention

Employee lying will likely occur in workplaces regardless of the effort put forth to stop it. However, the severity of dishonesty can be reduced using preventative measures.

The best methods for preventing employee lying include the following:

Perform background checks

This is the most important prevention method because, if done correctly, it stops liars from becoming employees. These checks can find out a lot of information about applicants...including their history of lying at previous jobs.

Three major background checks related to lying include:

Employment history

This indicates things an employee might have done that might not have been mentioned on a resume or during an interview. For obvious reasons, past lying is not something that most people would willingly divulge.

Academic history

Academic history is important because dishonest behavior discovered by universities or colleges is often a permanent part of a student's file. Again, this is something that most applicants would not want a potential employer to know.

Criminal history

This indicates evidence of lying in the past, but, more importantly, it shows any type of behavior that might lead to dishonesty.

Establish written policies

This is the easiest method of prevention because any organization can implement written policies. Policies set a clear tone of what is expected of employees. They promote positive behavior, discourage dishonesty, and outline discipline protocols for violating established rules.

These policies can be distributed to employees in a variety of ways. They can be handed out, emailed, or posted on employee bulletin boards. However, the best and most effective way to introduce them is during employee training or meetings. Employee signatures indicate they understand the rules involving dishonesty, and signatures are difficult to dispute when problems occur. This assures management that discipline can be taken without fear of future legal action.

Train employees

This is the most time-consuming and expensive method of prevention, but the payoff can be well worth it.

Training should start at orientation and be part of an ongoing process. It should also be two-fold, focusing on employees and supervision as follows:

Employee training

Make employees aware that there is no tolerance for dishonesty. Lying will be dealt with swiftly, and the punishment might include termination from the organization.

Also, encourage employees to report employee lies to supervisors. Let them know that their reporting will be taken seriously and kept in complete confidence.

In short, the most important aspects of this training are to (1) establish workplace dishonesty rules with consequences for violation and (2) build trust that management will react appropriately to any employee lying.

Supervisor training

Supervisors need to understand that part of their jobs involves keeping employees happy. Happy employees find job satisfaction, and they are less likely to lie.

Supervisors also need to be trained to listen to employee concerns and act accordingly. Their involvement is key to stopping lying and preventing it from reoccurring.

Take swift action for violations

At first glance, this method of prevention might appear to only be "after the fact" or reactive. However, this is not the case because swift action sets an example. Employees will be less likely to lie if they know they are going to be confronted and disciplined when caught in the act. In short, swift action establishes a precedence for workplace dishonesty

Summary

Employee lies are untruthful statements that are purposely made for some type of benefit or gain. In some situations, lies are accepted or expected, but most of the time they end up having a negative effect on the workplace environment.

Employees lie for a variety of reasons, but very few of these are justifiable. This book examines the reasons employees lie and methods for preventing them from doing so. It contains workplace examples for illustration and clarification, and it is written for easy understanding at all levels.

Congratulations! You now understand more about employee lies...an important aspect of organizational behavior.

Social Loafing

Summary

Introduction

What is social loafing? Max Ringlemann, an agricultural engineer from France, first introduced the phenomenon in 1913. He said social loafing occurs in groups. Specifically, in regards to accomplishing tasks and objectives, people give less effort working in groups than they give working alone.

Many people have experienced social loafing in educational settings...specifically undergraduate college courses. There often seems to be those one or two group members who want to do the minimum to get by, and this tends to annoy other affiliates since they have to carry extra weight. This is an age-old problem that has gone on since groups were formed.

Social loafing also occurs in organizations. However, it differs from education because it is more permanent. Students typically work together for a semester, and their groups disband when the course ends. Workplace teams often last longer... oftentimes until a project is completed. Worse yet, hardworking employees sometimes have to work with social loafers for many years after teams have disbanded. This is a constant reminder of the extra work they had to perform due to the social loafers' refusal to contribute their fair share.

Based on the above, it's rather easy to see that social loafing can produce some negative effects. However, before we get into these effects, we need to discuss the reasons why this phenomenon occurs. The following section looks at specific causes of social loafing.

Causes

Social loafing occurs for a variety of reasons. The following are some common causes of the phenomenon using organizational examples for support and clarification:

Cultural influence

Culture is the most influential aspect of some people's lives. Certain cultures encourage social loafing while others discourage it. The United States, for example, tends to promote social loafing in workplaces because the major focus is on individual accomplishments. Group accomplishments reflect the group as a whole, not the individual, and this holds less importance for many employees. Americans prefer the accolades that come with individual achievements, so they give more effort when working alone than they do when working in groups.

Asians, on the other hand, view group accomplishments differently. They are less likely to social loaf due to the value their culture places on group accomplishments. Asians feel the accomplishments of the team reflect on them personally, so they tend to work harder when collaborating with others.

Organizational example

Zachary is a vice president at the United States division of an international automotive supplier. He is working on a team project with four other vice presidents from divisions in Japan, China,

South Korea, and the Philippines. The team's goal is to find faster ways to get products to market using existing channels of distribution.

The team assembles and starts to assign tasks. The Japanese, Filipino, Chinese, and South Korean vice presidents all welcome the opportunity for involvement. Zachary gladly lets them take responsibility because his interest in this team project takes a back seat to a marketing plan that he is currently working on by himself. If he succeeds with the marketing plan, he will establish the respect and credibility necessary to make him a legitimate candidate for the US president's job when it becomes available next year. Success on the team project will credit the group as a whole, and it will not showcase Zachary's individual talents.

In short, the business culture of the United States promotes Zachary's behavior. He is more likely to be promoted based on his individual achievements, and this leads to his social loafing on the team.

Sucker influence

In general, people do not want to feel like they are being taken advantage of by others. In group settings, they avoid volunteering due to fear that others will stick them with the majority of the work. An example is a booster club for a boy's high school football team. Parents of the players are strongly encouraged to help out with booster club activities. However, very few parents volunteer because they do not want to end up doing the majority of the work. They believe that once they start taking on responsibilities, the coaches will assume that they can handle other tasks and ask them to do more.

Organizational example

Clara works as a salesperson at a window installation company. The company plans to have a holiday party for all employees and their families, and volunteers are needed to help organize the event. As a recruitment method, management sends out an email to all employees asking for their assistance. Clara wants to volunteer to set up the decorations, but she does not want this to lead to other duties being assigned to her. She is afraid that she will end up being responsible for food, entertainment, and clean-up for the party.

Ultimately, Clara decides to hold off on volunteering to avoid becoming a sucker. She becomes a social loafer so other employees are not able to take advantage of her.

Free-rider influence

Some individuals are aware that they will receive credit for the group performance regardless of their efforts, so they choose to take a free ride at the expense of others. An example of this involves a protest march. Everyone in the group marches to the point of destination, but some people choose not to speak up once they arrive. They simply sit back and watch while others voice their opinions about the cause. The non-vocal protesters receive credit for being part of the protest group, but they are not involved in some of the most important work because their efforts are not necessary.

Organizational example

Sara works at the headquarters of a retail clothing store chain. She is upset because management has decided that the company will no longer offer dental insurance to employees. She joins a group of 20 other employees who schedule a meeting with the president to discuss the loss of their dental program.

The group meets with the president in a conference room, but only four members speak up during the meeting (Sara is not one of them). They voice their displeasure with the change and, as a result, the president decides to extend dental coverage for another 60 days while management revisits the cost issue to see if the program can be continued.

This is a victory for the protesting group of employees, and Sara receives credit for being part of that group. However, she receives this credit without saying a word during the meeting.

Ultimately, four employees in the group did the majority of the work while the rest of the members were social loafers who benefitted as free riders.

Lack of significance

People become social loafers when they do not believe that their contributions matter. It's not that they don't care; it's that they don't believe effort on their part will make a difference.

One example of insignificance involves voting for people who have been nominated for a board of director positions at a large mutual fund. Small investors believe their votes will not make a difference, so they throw their ballots in the trash when they receive them. If those same investors were part of a 10-person committee that determined the board members' status, they likely would have taken their voting rights much more seriously.

Another example of insignificance involves boycotting. A woman might not like the fact that a worldwide tuna fish producer kills dolphins while fishing for tuna. However, the tuna company is so large that the woman believes her boycott of their tuna will not make any difference, so she continues to buy their products. If this woman bought her tuna directly from a local fisherman who killed dolphins while fishing, she would have been more likely to boycott his business.

Organizational example

Hargrove Manufacturing employs over 1200 people. The company is considering implementing a profit-sharing plan, and management has been asking for input from employees regarding their level of interest. So far, the comments have been overwhelmingly in favor of the plan. Over 450 employees have responded, and 95% like the idea.

Marcus is a production worker at the Hargrove, and he wants the profit-sharing plan to be implemented. However, after hearing about the large number of employees that have indicated they support the idea, he decides not to submit his own comments.

In short, Marcus is a social loafer because he does not believe his contributions will matter. He cares about the profit-sharing plan and wants it implemented, but he does not believe effort on his part is significant enough to make a difference in the outcome.

Lack of unity

Teams lack unity when members fail to bond and establish good working relationships. Lack of unity causes social loafing because members are not concerned with helping each other achieve the objectives of the team. An example is a church choir where the members do not get along with each other. Every time they hold a practice, at least two members do not show up. This is detrimental to the choir since their goal is to get better...and that will not happen if all members are not present. In short, the members who skip practice are not concerned about the choir due to the lack of unity within.

Organizational example

Renee works in quality control for a computer printer manufacturer. She has been assigned to a team with a production employee, a research & development employee, and an accounting employee. The goal of the team is to find areas where costs can be reduced in production.

The team has met twice a week for the past three weeks, but Renee has not established a comfort level at the meetings. She has not been able to bond with the other members, and this is causing her to lose interest in the cost savings objective of the team. She starts to focus on other job-related tasks that she finds more interesting, and the team moves to the backburner in terms of importance.

Renee is a social loafer because she has not been able to establish a good working relationship with the other members. This lack of unity causes her to lose interest in helping others achieve the goals of the team.

Lack of skills

When people work with others who lack skills, they are inclined to reduce their own performance and become social loafers. An example is a student who volunteers to work on the technical crew for the high school musical. He is very tech-savvy and wants to add a variety of technical effects to the performance. However, after meeting the rest of the technical crew, he realizes that none of them have achieved his level of skill and expertise, so he tones down his idea and makes the music much simpler in terms of technology.

Organizational example

Shannon is starting a new position as a laboratory supervisor. She has a very good understanding of laboratory procedures, and she plans to completely revamp the microbiological program by adding modern methodology and making it government-certified. However, after she starts her job, she realizes the existing lab technicians are not capable of taking the lab to the next level. She could hire more skilled personnel who understand her needs, but instead, she decides to make things easier on everyone by foregoing her idea of upgrading and certifying the microbiology program.

Shannon is a social loafer because she decided not to upgrade and certify the microbiology laboratory. She realized the skill level of her technicians was not equal to her own, so she chose to simplify matters and take an easier route.

Lack of ambition

Sometimes people's lack of ambition causes them to become social loafers. Their goal is to work as little as possible, and they plan accordingly to achieve that goal. An example is a football who fakes an injury during practice so he does not have to run for conditioning. He likes playing football, but he has no desire to run.

Organizational example

Stanley is a stock person at a hardware store. He does not really care about his job, has no desire to grow with the company, and does not plan to become a long-term employee. He remains employed at the hardware store because he needs money and has no desire to look elsewhere for a job.

Today a customer needs Stanley's assistance. She cannot find roofing nails, and she asks Stanley if the store has any in stock. Without bothering to look, Stanley tells her that everything they have is on the store shelf. In reality, there are five cases of roofing nails in the stockroom, but Stanley has no desire to retrieve them for the customer.

Stanley is a social loafer due to his lack of ambition. He does whatever is necessary to avoid work…even if it means lying to customers.

Lack of urgency

People who believe others are handling everything tend to relax and not contribute their fair share. They don't react until the situation becomes desperate or urgent…and this typically does not occur when other people are willing to do the work. An example is an adult male who still lives with his parents. His mother has cooked his meals and done his laundry for his entire life, so he can sit back and essentially do nothing. He will only need to contribute if his mother decides to stop doing the work for him…and this is likely not going to happen.

Organizational example

Melanie is a customer service representative at a windshield replacement company. A light bulb has burned out on her desk lamp. She knows a new bulb is located less than 100 feet away from her desk, but Instead of replacing it, she calls for maintenance.

Melanie is a social loafer because she knows the maintenance department will handle her problem. She will not replace the bulb herself if other people are available to do the work for her. If nobody is available and limited light prevents her from doing her work, then she will change the bulb.

Lack of monitoring

Many people need structure to be productive. Part of that structure involves monitoring of the activities they are performing…and that monitoring often comes in the form of supervision.

Lack of monitoring can create problems. An example includes a man who is running for a position in congress. He stops in Baltimore, Maryland to make a campaign speech. However, none of the people on his Baltimore team were instructed on how to prepare for his speech, so nothing is ready when he arrives. The entire staff social loafed because their preparation activities were not monitored.

Organizational example

Aaron works for a mortgage broker that strongly believes in teamwork when dealing with customers. He works with six other employees on a sales team, and their job is to contact potential customers for business.

The team reports to Helen, but she is out of the office most of the day. She checks back at the end of the day to review sales, but she is not actively involved in supervising her employees.

Aaron takes advantage of Helen's absence. He does personal work at his computer, takes extended lunches, and talks with other employees when he is supposed to be working. Due to Helen's lack of monitoring, Aaron is a social loafer.

Lack of compensation

Some people become social loafers when they believe they are not being equally compensated for their efforts. An example is a middle school student who receives worse grades than other students in her classroom. Her grades are upsetting to her, so she starts to withdraw and no longer participates in group discussions. Her perception of the situation and resulting attitude turn her into a social loafer.

Organizational example

Ann works with three other women in the office of a home insulation company. These ladies do general office work that includes answering phones and taking orders, and they report to the owner of the company Elisha.

Throughout the year, Elisha gives the office women rewards for doing a good job. Examples include gift certificates for massages or dinner, baseball or theater tickets, or $50 cash to spend on whatever they desire.

Ann has not received a reward from Elisha for the past nine months. All three other women have received awards during this time period, and this is upsetting to Ann. She feels like her efforts are being overlooked, and this causes her to do less work. She waits until one of the other ladies answers phone calls, and she does not volunteer to take on extra tasks during busy periods. In short, Ann's perceived lack of compensation causes her to become a social loafer.

Lack of contribution

It is fairly common for people to become social loafers when they believe that they are doing more work than others. They view other people as doing less work, and this causes them to lower their efforts as a form of retaliation. An example involves two boys, George and Andy, doing landscape work at their father's house. Andy stops work on two separate occasions to talk to his girlfriend on his cell phone. This upsets George because he continually works while Andy does little to contribute. During Andy's third phone call, George stops working and lies down on a hammock in an attempt to equalize the workload.

Organizational example

Gary is a commercial plumber. He is currently working on a big job with another plumber named Stephen. Over a two-week period, Stephen has left the work site more than five times to "check on a job" at a different location. Each time Stephen leaves, he is gone for more than two hours…and this is very upsetting to Gary because he is left alone to do the work.

One day, after Stephen returns from his "job check," Gary tells him that he has to work at a different location. He goes home and does not return for the rest of the day. This is Gary's way of retaliating for all the time that Stephen has missed.

In short, Gary became a social loafer due to Stephen's lack of contribution. The most interesting thing about this situation is that social loafing caused a person to become a social loafer.

Now you are aware of some common causes of social loafing. Next, let's move into the effects of these causes.

Effects

The previous section discussed the causes of social loafing. This section takes that discussion to the next level by examining the end results of this phenomenon. Specifically, it looks at the effects of social loafing in organizations. Please consider the following:

Cultural influence

Certain cultures promote individual accomplishments, while others promote group accomplishments. In workplaces, this is not fair to the individuals within those cultures for two reasons:

Unfair workloads

Employees from cultures that promote group accomplishments end up doing most of the work because employees from cultures that promote individual accomplishments give a limited effort.

Unbalanced input

Employees that participate can slant group decisions to benefit their cultures. Other cultures do not get an equal voice because their representative is a social loafer.

Sucker influence

The sucker influence can lead to some big problems. If every employee wants to avoid being the sucker, then they all become social loafers. When every worker's effort is reduced, nothing gets accomplished and the organization falls short of achieving goals and objectives.

Free-rider influence

Some workers free-ride because they know they will receive credit regardless of the amount of effort they put forth simply by being part of the group. Their effort is insignificant, so they sit back and watch others do the work.

Unfortunately, free-riding creates issues in organizations. People can turn free-riding into a habit, and then they never give an effort or accomplish anything. This is not good for the employee or the organization.

Lack of significance

Some employees choose not to contribute because they do not think their efforts will have any impact on the group outcome. If only one or two people choose to do this, their behavior might not pose a problem. However, if multiple people refrain from contributing, then group efficiency will suffer and objectives will be jeopardized.

Lack of unity

When groups do not have unity, members are not concerned with helping each other. This affects groups because they fail to meet objectives. When group objectives are not met, organizations fall short of accomplishing goals.

Lack of skills

This occurs when employees reduce their efforts because they believe others in their group have less skills than themselves. This is restricting to organizations because it prevents growth and progression. It can also result in the organization becoming less competitive...and ultimately ceasing to exist.

Lack of ambition

Some employees have a goal of doing as little work as possible, and they plan their day around achieving that goal. This can result in deceitful actions, such as lying, that negatively impact people and organizations. Additionally, employees who are known for lacking ambition can become outcasts in organizations because others do not want to work with them.

Lack of urgency

One problem with sitting back and relaxing while others do the work is that it can be very annoying to those shouldering the responsibilities. However, this is not the biggest concern. Waiting for a situation to become urgent before giving an effort can be disastrous because the delayed reaction can be too late. This means problems cannot be resolved...and the organization suffers from not achieving goals.

Lack of monitoring

Lack of monitoring results in a lack of structure...and environments that lack structure are excellent for social loafing. However, social loafing is not the biggest issue faced by an organization in this situation. A more prevalent concern is that lack of monitoring can lead to confusion and turmoil where nothing is organized and nothing gets accomplished. In short, a lack of monitoring can lead to chaos in workplaces that can be difficult to bring under control.

Lack of compensation

Employees sometimes social loaf because they feel they are not properly compensated for their efforts. They behave in this manner because they are demotivated by the unjust treatment. This negatively impacts many aspects of their jobs...including their performance. It can also cause them to leave the organization for employment elsewhere.

Lack of contribution

As a means of retaliation, some employees become social loafers when they believe they are doing more work than their coworkers. When this happens, everyone decreases their work effort and nothing gets accomplished. This creates an overall bad situation because employee attitudes decline, efficiency decreases, and organizational goals are not attained.

Based on the above, it's obvious that social loafing can damage organizations. That being said, there must be ways to prevent it....and those ways are discussed in the next section.

Prevention

Workplace social loafing needs to be prevented. Some of the best ways to do this include the following

Establish written procedures

This is the easiest method of prevention because any organization can implement written policies. Policies set a clear tone of what is expected of employees working together in teams. They need to know that social loafing will not be tolerated and there will be consequences for this type of behavior.

These policies can be distributed to employees in a variety of ways. They can be handed out, emailed, or posted on employee bulletin boards. However, the best and most effective way to introduce them is during employee training or meetings. Employee signatures indicate they understand the rules involving social loafing, and signatures are difficult to dispute when problems occur. This assures management that discipline can be taken without fear of future legal action.

Establish individual responsibilities

Employees need to know what is expected of them at work, and this applies when they are placed on teams. Expectations should be outlined before the team is assembled so members are not left guessing what they need to do. These responsibilities need to be clearly defined for easy understanding by the team members. This prevents social loafing because all team members have designated tasks that are solely their responsibility.

Scrutinize team member selection

Avoid hasty decisions when assigning people to teams by taking the time to examine employee backgrounds, skills, and accomplishments. Members need to be selected based on their knowledge and abilities, and thought should be given as to whether the team should be heterogeneous or homogeneous.

Also, avoid placing people on teams based on hierarchy status or structural charts. Some of the best teams include members from all levels and aspects of an organization. This allows for creative thinking, better problem solving, and the prevention of social loafing.

Scrutinize team sizes

Team size is another important concern. Teams that are too large tend to be cumbersome. Members spend a lot of time defining roles, assigning responsibilities, and resolving discrepancies. For instance, a team with 20 members would not work well for the design of a bicycle tire. Member's responsibilities would probably overlap, and social loafing would be likely to occur.

An obvious question arises from this team size discussion. What is the correct number of team members? This is a difficult question to answer, but a general rule of thumb is no less than four and no more than ten. This range provides the necessary expertise and is not likely to promote an environment of social loafing.

Provide feedback on team progress

Management needs to let teams know how they are progressing. Members need to know that they are on the right track with their ideas and solutions, and they should be recognized for their efforts. People like to be acknowledged when they are doing a good job, and this can be done using feedback.

Feedback can also be used to curb social loafing. Employees need to know when they are not contributing enough so they can make the necessary adjustments to improve. Once these weaknesses are brought out into the open, members who are contributing the most can offer encouragement to the loafers to make sure they stay on the right track. The idea is to encourage a solution-oriented group culture rather than a culture of blame.

Require team members to rate each other

Organizations can take a page from education for this prevention method. Employees on teams know which members are working and which members are loafing. Management needs to tap this knowledge to properly address social loafing issues. Once supervisors understand the inner workings of the team, they can "call out" those who give the least amount of effort. This stops slacking within the group, and it sends a message that social loafing will not be tolerated.

Promote a teamwork culture

A culture that promotes teamwork will prevent social loafing by encouraging everyone to help each other. However, leadership needs to be directly involved for this to happen. Culture starts at the top of an organization and works its way down into the rank and file. High-level personnel are the only people who have the authority and influence necessary to create a culture that promotes teamwork and prevents social loafing.

Summary

Social loafers are people who give less effort working with others than they do working alone. Unfortunately, this phenomenon has been experienced by most people simply because there are always individuals who want to avoid doing work.

Workplace social loafing has a variety of causes, and most of these causes produce negative effects. Groups fail to achieve established objectives, and this leads to organizations failing to achieve goals. Proactive organizations implement measures to prevent social loafing from occurring.

This book focuses on social loafing in organizations. Specifically, it examines the causes of social loafing in organizations, effects of social loafing in organizations, and methods for prevention of social loafing in organizations.

Congratulations! You now understand social loafing...an important aspect of organizational behavior.

Deviance

Introduction

The word "deviance" has a negative image associated with it for many people. This is because it refers to actions outside of established rules and regulations. Some deviance is worse than others, but it all violates some type of predetermined norms.

Workplace deviance is the purposeful act of harming employers and employees. These actions violate workplace standards, regulations, rules, and norms with the intent of doing mental or physical damage to people or organizations.

Employees become deviant due to their experiences in the workplace. They feel they have been improperly supervised, mistreated, or disrespected, and this leads them to take some type of retaliatory action. They might even do things they know are wrong just to see what they can get away with or for amusement purposes. Regardless of the reasons, employees behave in deviant ways that cause problems for people and organizations.

This book explores workplace deviance by explaining and exemplifying the concept. Organizational examples are used for clarification and illustration purposes, and the reader ends up with a greater understanding of this important aspect of organizational behavior.

Let's move on to the various types of deviant behavior found in workplaces.

Types

Employees engage in deviant behavior in a variety of ways. Sometimes this behavior is relatively harmless. Examples include mild gossip or taking an occasional extended break. However, it can also result in mental or physical harm. Examples include sexual harassment and physical fighting.

This section classifies types of workplace deviance. It simplifies understanding through categorization and explanation as follows:

Direct mental

Employees who exhibit direct mental deviant behavior have a direct impact on the organization and the mental well-being of other employees. This involves using verbal or non-verbal actions that violate company rules and regulations to get others to comply with something or prevent them from obtaining information.

Sexual harassment

This involves unwanted or unwelcome sexual advances or requests for sexual favors. Unfortunately, this is a common form of deviant behavior that is sometimes difficult to control.

Organizational example

Jenny works at a doctor's office as a nurse. She is very good at her job and is well-liked by the staff and patients. One of the physicians, who is also a partner at the practice, has been trying to get Jenny to go out with him for drinks or a night on the town. Unfortunately, Jenny has no interest in this doctor. He is married and much older, and Jenny is simply not attracted to him.

The offending doctor is persistent about getting Jenny to go out with him. He is not overly aggressive, but his behavior is completely unacceptable. Jenny is not the type to start a lawsuit, but instead chooses to leave the office and take a job as a nurse at a hospital.

The end result of the doctor's sexual harassment was the loss of a very good nurse. He was lucky because his practice could have been sued...but Jenny chose to leave the organization rather than take legal action. In short, the doctor's deviant behavior damaged an employee and his practice. Jenny left on bad terms, and the doctor's office lost a good worker.

Verbal aggressiveness

Verbal aggressiveness is a personal and psychological assault on an employee's mental well-being during workplace interaction.

Organizational example

Mark is a full-time college student who also works part-time as a stock person at a toy store. It's late November and the best-selling toys need to be on the shelves for customers to purchase for Christmas. Mark tries his best to keep the shelves stocked, but he forgets to put out the stuffed Santa Clause dolls...and these are a big seller during the Christmas holiday season.

Mark's boss Linda notices his mistake and becomes irate. She curses at him, calls him stupid, and tells him he should be fired for such a dumb error. Linda's personal attack makes Mark feel terrible. His morale greatly decreases, and he thinks about quitting. He also loses interest in making sure his job is done to the best of his ability, and this causes him to make a few more mistakes that Linda does not notice.

Linda's verbal aggressiveness is very demotivating. She chose to attack Mark instead of the problem, and this negatively impacted his attitude toward his job. In the end, Linda's deviant behavior had a negative impact on an employee and the toy store.

Threats

Threats are employees' indications that they intend to do some type of harm to other employees if they do not comply with certain demands.

Organizational example

Juan works at a paper mill. He notices a quality problem and wants to bring it to the attention of his supervisor. However, before he can do this, he is confronted by Peter...the employee who caused the quality error. Peter tells Juan that he is going to "beat him up after work" if the supervisor finds out. Juan fears for his physical health and safety, so he decides to keep the quality problem to himself.

In this case, Peter's threat worked well. It prevented Juan from going to his supervisor with a problem. However, this deviant behavior resulted in two rather serious issues. First, Juan will never report quality mistakes to his supervisor due to the fear of getting beat up. Second, the organization is releasing inferior products into commerce because management is not aware of the problem. The end result is a loss for the employee and the paper mill.

Hostility

Hostility involves employees' unfriendly actions or attitudes toward other employees. The intent is to show dislike for an organization or an employee.

Organizational example

Rhonda is a stewardess for an airline. She enjoys working on international flights because she gets to travel to different countries. She is typically in a good mood, and she is well-liked by customers and coworkers.

Harvey works as a steward for the same airline as Rhonda. He also likes to work on international flights. However, he thinks the airline should pay him more money, so he bears a grudge against the organization. This grudge is evident whenever Harvey works a flight. He is downright mean to his coworkers. He is rude, cruel, insulting, and has a generally mean disposition.

Rhonda strongly dislikes working with Harvey due to his rudeness and hostility toward her. She dislikes him so much that she gets physically ill when she is scheduled to work with him, and she sometimes is forced to use a sick day due to her illness.

In this situation, Harvey's hostility is detrimental. His deviant behavior affects the organization and employees. Rhonda is so distressed by him that she is forced to call in sick and loses pay, and the airline misses a good employee when she is not working.

Silence

This involves choosing to intentionally remain silent to withhold information that other employees might find useful. This is often done for job security reasons.

Organizational example

Cindy is a CPA at an accounting firm. She has been with the firm for five years, and she has picked up some important clients during that time.

Cindy believes that information is power. She does not share anything about her clients with other accountants because she feels she is more valuable to the firm if nobody else has the knowledge that she possesses.

Cindy might have a legitimate point about being more valuable by withholding information, but this is not good for other accountants or the firm. When she goes on vacation or takes other time off, other accountants are left in the dark about her clients. They have to call her at home or contact the customer if they need information, and this takes time and effort that would not be required if Cindy shared information.

In this case, Cindy's silence damages employees and the organization. Other accountants have to do more work than should be necessary to get information, and this costs the accounting firm time and money. In short, Cindy's deviant behavior hurts the accounting firm when she takes time off....and the damage could be much more serious if she decides to leave the organization.

Indirect mental

Employees who exhibit indirect mental deviant behavior have an indirect impact on the organization and the mental well-being of other employees. This involves using verbal or non-verbal actions that violate company rules and regulations to avoid work, make statements, express opinions, or prevent others from progressing.

Rumors

Rumors are stories or reports about employees or the organization that might or might not be truthful. Typically, rumors focus more on organizational happenings or actions.

Organizational example

Elliot works as a loan processor at a bank. One of his customers tells him that his bank might be for sale, and he is intent on sharing this information with other employees.

As Elliot comes in contact with his coworkers, he tells them the story he heard from his customer. This story might or might not be true, but employees fear for their jobs when they hear it. Some employees start to look for other jobs, and two tellers leave the organization to take similar positions with another bank.

The sale rumor spread by Elliot negatively impacted the bank regardless of the truth involved. It resulted in employees fearing for their jobs, and some workers started to look for other positions. Two tellers left to take employment with a competitor. In short, Elliot's deviant behavior caused employees to worry...possibly unnecessarily, and it also resulted in the bank losing two good employees.

Gossip

Gossip involves telling stories about employees or the organization that might or might not be truthful. Typically, gossip focuses more on employee happenings or actions.

Organizational example

Leslie is a secretary at an automotive dealer who enjoys any type of gossip. Recently, she heard that Bill, one of the salespeople, was having an affair with one of his customers. This is very interesting to Leslie because Bill and the customer are both married...but not to each other.

Leslie begins to ask every coworker she encounters if they know anything about the affair. None of the employees she talks with seem to know any details, but news of the affair spreads like wildfire through the dealership. Some employees are so upset with Bill that they give him "the cold shoulder" when they see him. One salesperson who was going to utilize Bill in for his sales expertise decides to ask someone else for help. This decision costs Bill almost 400 dollars in commission.

The affair story that Leslie spread around the dealership was detrimental to Bill. Her deviant behavior cost him money and caused other employees to ignore him. The worst part about this situation is the fact that there is no proof of the affair being true...it is merely based on gossip.

Backstabbing

Backstabbing is the act of criticizing or attacking another employee while faking that a friendship exists. This is a deceptive form of workplace deviance that often blindsides coworkers.

Organizational example

Nicholas and Anita work as cake decorators at an upscale bakery. Anita has been working on an elaborate wedding cake for the past week. She believes she is finished with the project, but she asks Nicholas for his opinion before she releases the cake to the customer.

Nicholas looks at the cake and immediately notices that the spelling of the bride's name is wrong. Her name is "Denise," and Anita has written "Dennis." Instead of pointing this error out, Nicholas puts his arm around Anita and tells her that she did a great job. He also tells her that he is glad he met her and truly respects her because she is such a professional and a good friend.

In this situation, Nicholas saw a mistake that he knew would upset the bride. Instead of telling Anita about the problem, he told her the cake looked great and expressed gratitude for her friendship. Nicholas backstabbed Anita while faking a friendship, and this deviant behavior will cause a problem with the customer on her wedding day.

Loafing

Loafing is avoiding work while other employees do more than their fair share by "picking up the slack."

Organizational example

Deanna and George are part of a research team trying to gather information on heart attack prevention for the National Health Association (NHA). The team has seven members, but Deanna and George are doing the vast majority of the work. Other team members state that they cannot find time to help because they have other obligations that require their time.

Deanna and George are fairly good-natured about this situation until the president of NHA decides to recognize the entire team for the excellent work they have done. Every member takes credit for Deanna and George's work, and this upsets both of them. They complain to other employees in the organization about the work they have done and the fact that other team members unfairly received credit for the team's success. Their attitudes deteriorate, and they eventually give less effort for every work-related task they perform.

Deanna and George were resentful of the social loafers and the president, and this had a negative impact on their morale. This problem was a direct result of deviant behavior by five team members.

Favoritism

Favoritism is the act of favoring one employee at the expense of another. Typically, favoritism comes from management rather than coworkers.

Organizational example

Wanda is an accountant at a telephone service company. She has worked for the organization for nine years, is typically upbeat and happy, and is well-liked by management and coworkers.

The president of the company announces that the controller's position is now open because the current controller is retiring. Wanda applies for this job, but it is ultimately given to another accountant who has less experience than Wanda, but is a personal friend of the president.

Wanda is upset that she was passed over for the controller's position, and it shows in her attitude. Coworkers frequently hear her saying that she does not care what happens in the organization, and she no longer seems happy at work. This is a big difference from the way she was before she was passed over for the promotion.

Wanda's disappointment about not getting the controller's position shows in her negative attitude, and it is a direct result of the president's deviant behavior.

Physical

Employees who exhibit this behavior have an indirect impact on the physical well-being of products, equipment, buildings, or other employees. This involves taking physical action that violates company rules and regulations to make statements, express discontent, prevent productivity, control others, or gain something personally.

Property damage

Property damage is the act of destroying equipment, buildings, or property as a means of retaliation or making a statement. This type of action is not only deviant, but it can also result in legal action from the employer.

Organizational example

Tony works as a typesetter at a printer. He believes he works very hard and does not get properly compensated for his efforts. He has tried to unionize his fellow workers, but was unsuccessful....and this added to his frustration.

One night, under the cover of darkness, Tony parks his car in a lot about three blocks from the printer. He sneaks through back alleys to get to his place of employment and promptly begins to write negative messages about management on the outside of the building. He writes "terrible bosses" and "this place sucks" with black spray paint.

When employees come to work the next day, they are shocked. Management is very upset, and they have to hire an outside company to remove the graffiti. Tony's deviant behavior damaged the printer's image and cost money to clean the building.

Product sabotage

Product sabotage occurs when employees deliberately manipulate an organization's products so they cause damage to consumers or render the products unusable. This is done for retaliation or anger reasons.

Organizational example

Chelsea works for a meat processor packing ham and sausage products. She is upset because her supervisor will not let her transfer to another job that she perceives as easier than her current position.

One particular day, Chelsea gets into an argument with one of her coworkers. This adds to her mounting frustration, so she decides to get even with the company. She deliberately places a piece of hard plastic in one of the packages of ham. She knows that any customer who bites this plastic will surely be upset, and he or she could issue a complaint that damages the image of the organization.

Chelsea's product sabotage could have a very negative impact on the meat processor. She is exposing them to a potential food safety issue, and it could result in the United States Department of Agriculture (USDA) shutting down the facility. In this case, Chelsea's deviant behavior could do major damage to the organization and the people employed by it.

Theft

Theft is the act of taking something that belongs to other employees or the organization. It is done for personal gain.

Organizational example

Norman works as a quality control technician at a bottle manufacturer. In his spare time, he likes to experiment with cooking. He has a variety of cookbooks, and many of them require weighing ingredients for accuracy.

At work, Norman has access to various areas of the plant...including the laboratory. He notices a small scale in the lab that would be perfect for his cooking hobby, and he takes it home without anyone's permission.

Eventually, the laboratory manager notices the scale is missing. She questions the lab technicians about its whereabouts, but none of them know what happened...so she has to order a new scale as a replacement. The new scale costs the bottle manufacturer 150 dollars, and it is a direct result of Norman's deviant behavior.

Fighting

Fighting is the act of engaging in a physical confrontation with another employee. This is used for compliance gaining purposes, and it is also a reaction to anger.

Organizational example

Oswald is a shipping and receiving clerk at a furniture warehouse. He likes his job, but does not like it when other shipping employees tell him that he has made a mistake.

Dominic, another employee in the shipping department, notices that there is an error in an order put up for an important customer. He finds out that Oswald made the mistake, and confronts him about it. Oswald is offended, heated words are exchanged, and the two men end up in a physical fight.

After reviewing the situation, management at the furniture warehouse decides to terminate both employees for fighting. Oswald and Dominic both lose their jobs, and the furniture warehouse has to replace and train two new receiving employees. The loss is substantial, and it is a direct result of workplace deviance.

Performance

Employees who exhibit performance-based deviant behavior have an indirect impact on the workload of other employees and the efficiency of the organization. This involves taking action that violates company rules and regulations to make statements, express discontent, prevent productivity, increase others' workloads, or gain something personally.

Extended breaks

This is taking breaks that are longer than expected or granted by the organization. It involves doing non-work-related things at a time that the organization expects work-related tasks to be performed. It is done for personal reasons or to avoid work.

Organizational example

Penelope is an office worker at an insurance company. She does her job well, but she has a habit of taking extra time at breaks to talk with other employees. This causes a problem because she answers phones and another employee needs to replace her during her breaks. The replacement employee has his own work to do, and Penelope's lack of consideration upsets him because he falls behind on his own job.

Penelope takes advantage of the organization by extending her breaks to talk with other employees. Her lack of courtesy also upsets her replacement because he falls behind on his job responsibilities. These problems are the direct result of Penelope's deviant workplace behavior.

Leaving early

This involves leaving work at an earlier time than expected by the organization. It is done for personal reasons or to avoid work.

Organizational example

Pueblo is the first shift manager at a hardware store. He is well-liked by customers and his employees, but he often leaves the store 10 or 15 minutes before the end of his shift. This causes a problem because he is not present for a smooth transition to the next shift, and that upsets the second shift manager.

Pueblo takes advantage of the organization by leaving early. He also puts an unfair burden on the second shift manager who is forced to oversee the transition between shifts. These problems are the direct result of Pueblo's deviant behavior.

Arriving late

This involves arriving at work at a later time than expected by the organization. It is done for personal reasons or to avoid work.

Organizational example

Ellen is an attorney at a law firm. She performs her job well, but she has a problem showing up for work on time. Her start time, established by the partners at the firm, is 8:00 am, but she rarely gets to work before 8:30 am.

The partners at the law firm have talked to Ellen about her tardiness, but she does not change. She does not see a problem with being a little late as long as she performs her job well. However, the partners do not share the same viewpoint, and this creates a problem.

When bonuses come at the end of the year, Ellen's is less than the other attorneys. She is upset over this and asks the partners why she was slighted. They explain that she never started work at the agreed-upon hours, and this was taken into account. Ellen is not happy with this explanation, and she abruptly quits the firm to look for other employment.

In the end, Ellen's deviant behavior was damaging to herself and the law firm. She quit a job that provided a fairly comfortable living, and the law firm lost a good employee.

Calling in sick

This involves missing a scheduled day of work. It is done for personal reasons or to avoid work.

Organizational example

Hillary is a cabinet assembler at a kitchen and bath remodeler. She does a very good job from a quality aspect and is well-liked by her coworkers. One problem with Hillary, however, is the fact that she calls in sick about twice per month. She does not get paid for these days, but it adds work for the other cabinet assemblers and sometimes they fall behind on orders.

Regardless of the quality of Hillary's work, she is of no value to the organization if she is not present. Her deviant behavior forces others to do more work, and it hurts the organization because they cannot properly fill customer orders.

Causes

Poor supervision

Poor supervision comes from management, and it causes employees to become deviant as a means of retaliation or protest.

This might be the most common cause of deviant behavior due to power imbalances. Employees do not have equal levels of power with their supervisors from a hierarchy standpoint, so they find other ways to express their discontent or unhappiness.

Disrespect

Disrespects typically comes from the way employees treat coworkers. It causes employees to become deviant as a means of fighting back or showing that they are not going to take it.

This might be the most serious cause of deviant behavior because it can lead to physical confrontations. People who believe they are being personally disrespected often confront the responsible employee...and this can lead to fighting. As a result, both employees can lose their jobs causing the employees and the organization to suffer.

Mistreatment

Mistreatment comes from the way employees treat coworkers. It can cause employees to become deviant as a means of retaliation, frustration, or anger.

Often times employees who believe they are being mistreated end up leaving the organization. If these employees are good at their jobs, then the organization loses twice...first from the deviant behavior and second from losing a valuable employee.

Amusement

Amusement typically results from boredom. It can cause employees to become deviant for fun, to see what will happen, or to see what they can get away with.

This is the most difficult cause of deviant behavior because there is no legitimate reason for the employee's actions...so it is difficult to establish a method of prevention.   Additionally, these employees are not necessarily unhappy, so they remain with the organization and continue their deviant ways.

Prevention

Open door policies

This is the most obvious method of prevention. Management needs to be involved if they want to prevent workplace deviance. They must encourage employees to come forward when they witness any type of deviant behavior. This can be done through meetings, emails, or suggestion boxes...the point is simply to get employees to point out problems and suggest solutions.

Additionally, employees who report deviances issues to management must have trust that their discussions will be kept in confidence. Employees who do not have trust will not expose problems.

Finally, leaders who are made aware of deviance issues need to act swiftly to stop them and prevent future reoccurrences. This shows that they support their employees, and want the workplace to be deviance free.

In short, management needs to be committed to preventing workplace deviance by actively encouraging employees to point out problems and make suggestions. If leaders do not prioritize deviance prevention, then employees will not sense seriousness and will not come forward with problems they observe.

Hiring practices

This is the most important prevention method because, if done correctly, it stops problem people from becoming employees.

Every employer should conduct background checks on people before hiring them. These checks can find out a lot of information about individuals...including their history of deviant behavior at previous jobs. Three major checks related to workplace deviance include:

Criminal history

This indicates past crimes committed, but, more importantly, it shows any type of anti-social behavior that might be workplace-related.

Employer history

This indicates things an employee might have done that might not have been mentioned on a resume or during an interview. For obvious reasons, past workplace deviance is not something that most people would willingly divulge.

Academic history

Academic history is important because deviant behavior discovered by universities or colleges is often a permanent part of a student's file. Again, this is something that most people would not want a potential employer to know.

Orientations and training

This is the most time-consuming and expensive method of prevention. However, if done properly, the payback is well worth it.

Training should start at orientation and be part of an ongoing process. It should also be two-fold, focusing on employees and supervision as follows:

Employee training

Make employees aware that there is no tolerance for deviant behavior. Any workplace deviance will be dealt with swiftly, and the punishment might include termination from the organization.

Also, encourage employees to report deviant behavior to supervisors. Let them know that their reporting will be taken seriously and kept in complete confidence.

In short, the most important aspects of this training are to (1) establish workplace deviance rules with consequences for violation and (2) build trust that management will react appropriately to any deviant behavior.

Supervisor training

Supervisors need to understand that part of their jobs involves keeping employees happy. Happy employees find job satisfaction, and they are less likely to participate in deviant behavior.

Supervisors also need to be trained to listen to employee concerns and act accordingly. Their involvement is key to stopping workplace deviance and preventing it from reoccurring.

Written policies

This is the easiest method of prevention because any organization can implement written policies. Policies set a clear tone of what is expected of employees. They promote positive behavior, discourage deviance, and outline discipline protocols for violating established rules.

These policies can be distributed to employees in a variety of ways. They can be handed out, emailed, or posted on employee bulletin boards. However, the best and most effective way to introduce them is during employee training or meetings. Employee signatures indicate they understand the rules involving workplace deviance, and signatures are difficult to dispute when problems occur. This assures management that discipline can be taken without fear of future legal action.

Summary

Workplace deviance is the intentional act of harming employers and employees. It violates workplace standards, regulations, rules, and norms, and it is a real concern for leadership of organizations. The effects can be long-lasting, and the impact can be devastating.

This book focuses on workplace deviance. Specifically, it examines the effect it has on people and organizations, the root causes, and the methods available for prevention. Simple explanations and related organizational examples are used for easy understanding, and this results in an informed reader at any educational level.

Congratulations! You now understand workplace deviance…a very important aspect of organizational behavior.

www.ingramcontent.com/pod-product-compliance
Lightning Source LLC
Chambersburg PA
CBHW070227210526
45169CB00023B/1173